2003

JANUARY

S	M	T	W	T	F	S
			1	2	3	4
5	6	7	8	9	10	11
12	13	14	15	16	17	18
19	20	21	22	23	24	25
26	27	28	29	30	31	

FEBRUARY

S	M	T	W	T	F	S
						1
2	3	4	5	6	7	8
9	10	11	12	13	14	15
16	17	18	19	20	21	22
23	24	25	26	27	28	

						1
2	3	4	5	6	7	8
9	10	11	12	13	14	15
16	17	18	19	20	21	22
23	24	25	26	27	28	29
30	31					

APRIL

S	M	T	W	T	F	S
		1	2	3	4	5
6	7	8	9	10	11	12
13	14	15	16	17	18	19
20	21	22	23	24	25	26
27	28	29	30			

MAY

S	M	T	W	T	F	S
				1	2	3
4	5	6	7	8	9	10
11	12	13	14	15	16	17
18	19	20	21	22	23	24
25	26	27	28	29	30	31

JUNE

S	M	T	W	T	F	S
1	2	3	4	5	6	7
8	9	10	11	12	13	14
15	16	17	18	19	20	21
22	23	24	25	26	27	28
29	30					

JULY

S	M	T	W	T	F	S
		1	2	3	4	5
6	7	8	9	10	11	12
13	14	15	16	17	18	19
20	21	22	23	24	25	26
27	28	29	30	31		

AUGUST

S	M	T	W	T	F	S
					1	2
3	4	5	6	7	8	9
10	11	12	13	14	15	16
17	18	19	20	21	22	23
24	25	26	27	28	29	30
31						

SEPTEMBER

S	M	T	W	T	F	S
	1	2	3	4	5	6
7	8	9	10	11	12	13
14	15	16	17	18	19	20
21	22	23	24	25	26	27
28	29	30				

OCTOBER

S	M	T	W	T	F	S
			1	2	3	4
5	6	7	8	9	10	11
12	13	14	15	16	17	18
19	20	21	22	23	24	25
26	27	28	29	30	31	

NOVEMBER

S	M	T	W	T	F	S
						1
2	3	4	5	6	7	8
9	10	11	12	13	14	15
16	17	18	19	20	21	22
23	24	25	26	27	28	29
30						

DECEMBER

S	M	T	W	T	F	S
	1	2	3	4	5	6
7	8	9	10	11	12	13
14	15	16	17	18	19	20
21	22	23	24	25	26	27
28	29	30	31			

PERSONAL NOTES

NAME . . . .

ADDRESS . . . .

. . . .

. . . .

. . . .

TELEPHONE (PRIVATE) . . . .

TELEPHONE (BUSINESS) . . . .

TELEPHONE (MOBILE) . . . .

FAX . . . .

E-MAIL . . . .

NOTES . . . .

. . . .

. . . .

. . . .

. . . .

. . . .

. . . .

If this Diary is found, please return to the owner at the above address

the TOLKIEN DIARY 2003

Illustrated by

Ted Nasmith

HarperCollins*Publishers*

HarperCollins*Publishers*
77-85 Fulham Palace Road
Hammersmith,
London W6 8JB
www.tolkien.co.uk

Published by HarperCollins*Publishers* 2002
The Tolkien Diary 2003

Original front cover design: Ted Nasmith
Design: Amzie Viladot Lorente

ISBN 0 00 711187 8

Printed and bound in Belgium by Proost NV, Turnhout

THE TOLKIEN SOCIETY
Details of the Tolkien Society can be obtained by sending a stamped addressed envelope, or (from outside the UK) an international reply paid coupon, to:

The Tolkien Society (HC),
65 Wentworth Crescent,
Ash Vale, Surrey GU12 5LF
England
E-mail: tolksoc@tolkiensociety.org
Website: http://www.tolkiensociety.org

WORKS BY J.R.R. TOLKIEN

THE HOBBIT
LEAF BY NIGGLE
ON FAIRY-STORIES
FARMER GILES OF HAM
THE HOMECOMING OF BEORHTNOTH
THE LORD OF THE RINGS
THE ADVENTURES OF TOM BOMBADIL
THE ROAD GOES EVER ON (WITH DONALD SWANN)
SMITH OF WOOTTON MAJOR

WORKS PUBLISHED POSTHUMOUSLY

SIR GAWAIN AND THE GREEN KNIGHT, PEARL AND SIR ORFEO
THE FATHER CHRISTMAS LETTERS
THE SILMARILLION
PICTURES BY J.R.R. TOLKIEN
UNFINISHED TALES
THE LETTERS OF J.R.R. TOLKIEN
FINN AND HENGEST
MR BLISS
THE MONSTERS AND THE CRITICS AND OTHER ESSAYS
ROVERANDOM

THE HISTORY OF MIDDLE-EARTH

BY CHRISTOPHER TOLKIEN

I THE BOOK OF LOST TALES, PART ONE
II THE BOOK OF LOST TALES, PART TWO
III THE LAYS OF BELERIAND
IV THE SHAPING OF MIDDLE-EARTH
V THE LOST ROAD AND OTHER WRITINGS
VI THE RETURN OF THE SHADOW
VII THE TREASON OF ISENGARD
VIII THE WAR OF THE RING
IX SAURON DEFEATED
X MORGOTH'S RING
XI THE WAR OF THE JEWELS
XII THE PEOPLES OF MIDDLE-EARTH

THE TWO TOWERS

'Three Rings for the Elven-kings under the sky,
Seven for the Dwarf-lords in their halls of stone,
Nine for Mortal Men doomed to die,
One for the Dark Lord on his dark throne
In the Land of Mordor where the Shadows lie.
One Ring to rule them all, One Ring to find them,
One Ring to bring them all and in the darkness bind them
In the Land of Mordor where the Shadows lie.'

'Among the greatest works of imaginative fiction of the twentieth century'
SUNDAY TELEGRAPH

The Two Towers is the second part of J.R.R. Tolkien's epic adventure, *The Lord of the Rings*.

Frodo and the Companions of the Ring have been beset by danger during their quest to prevent the Ruling Ring from falling into the hands of the Dark Lord by destroying it in the Cracks of Doom. They have lost the wizard, Gandalf, in the battle with an evil spirit in the Mines of Moria; and at the falls of Rauros, Boromir, seduced by the power of the Ring, tried to seize it by force. While Frodo and Sam made their escape the rest of the company were attacked by orcs.

Now they continue their journey alone down the great River Anduin – alone, that is, save for the mysterious creeping figure that follows wherever they go.

'Tolkien's invention of strange peoples, curious incidents, miraculous doings, is poured out in this second volume of his trilogy as exuberantly and convincingly, in a dreamlike way, as ever. As the story goes on the world of the Ring grows more vast and mysterious and crowded with curious figures, horrible, delightful or comic. The story itself is superb.'
THE OBSERVER

J.R.R. TOLKIEN

John **Ronald Reuel Tolkien** was born on 3rd January 1892 in Bloemfontein in the Orange Free State.

In early 1895 his mother, Mabel, returned to England with Ronald and his younger brother, Hilary, exhausted by the climate. After his father's death from rheumatic fever, the family made their home at Sarehole, near Birmingham. This beautiful rural area made a great impression on the young Ronald, and its effect can clearly be seen in his later writing and in his pictures.

Mabel died in 1904, leaving the boys to the care of Father Francis Morgan, a priest at the Birmingham Oratory. At King Edward's School, Ronald developed his linguistic talent and later began to invent languages of his own.

1914 saw the outbreak of the First World War. Ronald was in his final year at Oxford. He graduated the following year with a First in English language and literature and at once took up his commission as a second lieutenant in the Lancashire Fusiliers. Before embarking for France in 1916, he married his childhood sweetheart, Edith Bratt. Tolkien survived the Battle of the Somme but later that year he was struck down by trench fever and was invalided home.

The years after the war were devoted to his work as Professor of Anglo-Saxon at Oxford, where he was soon to prove himself one of the finest philologists in the world. He had already started to write the great cycle of myths and legends which was to become THE SILMARILLION. He and Edith had four children and it was for them that he first told the tale of THE HOBBIT, which was published in 1937 by Sir Stanley Unwin. It was so successful that the publisher immediately wanted a sequel, but it was not until 1954 that the first volume of his great masterpiece, THE LORD OF THE RINGS, was published to instant acclaim. Its enormous popularity took Tolkien by surprise.

After retirement Ronald and Edith Tolkien moved to Bournemouth, but when Edith died in 1971, Tolkien returned to Oxford. He died after a brief illness on 2nd September 1973.

TED NASMITH

Ted Nasmith has had a passionate interest in Tolkien since about 1970, even before he embarked on a career as an illustrator, having first read THE LORD OF THE RINGS as a young art student. It would be several years after he began making drawings and paintings from THE LORD OF THE RINGS and THE HOBBIT, however, before it would become the artistic mainstay it is currently. Instead, he found himself apprenticing as an architectural renderer, soon gaining a reputation for his high realism and dedication.

He now divides his time between architecture, Tolkien, and other types of illustration, but Tolkien has emerged as the predominant influence. With dozens of high realism gouache scenes painted over some 30 years, he has gained a worldwide reputation in the genre. His work has been published in several Tolkien calendars since 1987, but also in other forms; the recent illustrated edition of THE SILMARILLION being a particular honour.

His approach to illustrating Tolkien draws on influences such as 19th century 'old school' landscape and classical painting, as well as 'magic realism', fairy painting, the classic illustrators, and the visionary/psychedelic art of the 1960s.

Besides the sheer pleasure of bringing Tolkien's world to light, he sees his fantasy art as a bridge between the realm of 'everyday' and 'faerie', faerie being Tolkien's term for the enchanted world of our dreams and nightmares; that great ancient realm of Story.

He is currently at work on a new set of paintings for the 2004 Tolkien diary, THE RETURN OF THE KING.

January

BOROMIR'S LAST STAND

Then Boromir had come leaping through the trees. He had made them fight. He slew many of them and the rest fled. But they had not gone far on the way back when they were attacked again, by a hundred Orcs at least, some of them very large, and they shot a rain of arrows: always at Boromir. Boromir had blown his great horn till the woods rang, and at first the Orcs had been dismayed and had drawn back; but when no answer but the echoes came, they had attacked more fiercely than ever. Pippin did not remember much more.

[*The Uruk-hai*]

December 2002

MONDAY 23

Weeks 0 – 1

December

S	M	T	W	T	F	S
1	2	3	4	5	6	7
8	9	10	11	12	13	14
15	16	17	18	19	20	21
22	23	24	25	26	27	28
29	30	31				

TUESDAY 24

WEDNESDAY 25

Christmas Day

THURSDAY 26

Boxing Day
St. Stephen's Day (Rep. of Ireland)
Day of Goodwill (South Africa)

FRIDAY 27

SATURDAY 28

SUNDAY 29

January 2003

MONDAY 30

TUESDAY 31

WEDNESDAY 1
New Year's Day

THURSDAY 2
● (New Moon)

FRIDAY 3
J.R.R. Tolkien born, 1892

SATURDAY 4

SUNDAY 5

January

S	M	T	W	T	F	S
			1	2	3	4
5	6	7	8	9	10	11
12	13	14	15	16	17	18
19	20	21	22	23	24	25
26	27	28	29	30	31	

January

MONDAY 6
Epiphany

TUESDAY 7

WEDNESDAY 8

THURSDAY 9

Weeks 2 – 3

FRIDAY 10
◐ (First Quarter)

SATURDAY 11

SUNDAY 12

January

S	M	T	W	T	F	S
			1	2	3	4
5	6	7	8	9	10	11
12	13	14	15	16	17	18
19	20	21	22	23	24	25
26	27	28	29	30	31	

January

MONDAY 13

TUESDAY 14

WEDNESDAY 15

THURSDAY 16

FRIDAY 17

SATURDAY 18

○ (Full Moon)

SUNDAY 19

January

S	M	T	W	T	F	S
			1	2	3	4
5	6	7	8	9	10	11
12	13	14	15	16	17	18
19	20	21	22	23	24	25
26	27	28	29	30	31	

January

MONDAY 20
Martin Luther King Jr. Day (US)

Weeks 4 – 5

TUESDAY 21

WEDNESDAY 22

THURSDAY 23

FRIDAY 24

SATURDAY 25
◐ (Last Quarter)

SUNDAY 26
Australia Day (Aus)

January

S	M	T	W	T	F	S
			1	2	3	4
5	6	7	8	9	10	11
12	13	14	15	16	17	18
19	20	21	22	23	24	25
26	27	28	29	30	31	

February

MONDAY 27

TUESDAY 28

WEDNESDAY 29

THURSDAY 30

FRIDAY 31

SATURDAY 1

Chinese New Year/ ● (New Moon)

SUNDAY 2

February

S	M	T	W	T	F	S
						1
2	3	4	5	6	7	8
9	10	11	12	13	14	15
16	17	18	19	20	21	22
23	24	25	26	27	28	

February

FANGORN FOREST

He led the way in under the huge branches of the trees. Old beyond guessing, they seemed. Great trailing beards of lichen hung from them, blowing and swaying in the breeze. Out of the shadows the hobbits peeped, gazing back down the slope: little furtive figures that in the dim light looked like elf-children in the deeps of time peering out of the Wild Wood in wonder at their first Dawn.

[*The Uruk-hai*]

Ted Nasmith

February

MONDAY 3

TUESDAY 4

WEDNESDAY 5

THURSDAY 6
Waitangi Day (NZ)

Weeks 6 – 7

FRIDAY 7

SATURDAY 8

SUNDAY 9
◐ (First Quarter)

February

S	M	T	W	T	F	S
						1
2	3	4	5	6	7	8
9	10	11	12	13	14	15
16	17	18	19	20	21	22
23	24	25	26	27	28	

February

MONDAY 10

TUESDAY 11

WEDNESDAY 12
Lincoln's Birthday (US)
Eid-al-Adha

THURSDAY 13

FRIDAY 14
St. Valentine's Day

SATURDAY 15

SUNDAY 16
○ (Full Moon)

February

S	M	T	W	T	F	S
						1
2	3	4	5	6	7	8
9	10	11	12	13	14	15
16	17	18	19	20	21	22
23	24	25	26	27	28	

February

MONDAY 17
Presidents' Day (US)

Weeks 8 – 9

TUESDAY 18

WEDNESDAY 19

THURSDAY 20

FRIDAY 21

SATURDAY 22
Washington's Birthday (US)

SUNDAY 23
◐ (Last Quarter)

February

S	M	T	W	T	F	S
						1
2	3	4	5	6	7	8
9	10	11	12	13	14	15
16	17	18	19	20	21	22
23	24	25	26	27	28	

March

MONDAY 24

TUESDAY 25

WEDNESDAY 26

THURSDAY 27

FRIDAY 28

SATURDAY 1

St. David's Day (Wales)

SUNDAY 2

March

S	M	T	W	T	F	S
						1
2	3	4	5	6	7	8
9	10	11	12	13	14	15
16	17	18	19	20	21	22
23	24	25	26	27	28	29
30	31					

March

THE RIDERS OF ROHAN

Their horses were of great stature, strong and clean-limbed; their grey coats glistened, their long tails flowed in the wind... The Men that rode them matched them well: tall and long-limbed; their hair, flaxen-pale, flowed under their light helms, and streamed in long braids behind them; their faces were stern and keen. In their hands were tall spears of ash, painted shields were slung at their backs, long swords were at their belts, their burnished shirts of mail hung down upon their knees.

[*The Riders of Rohan*]

March

MONDAY 3
● (New Moon)

Weeks 10 – 11

March

S	M	T	W	T	F	S
						1
2	3	4	5	6	7	8
9	10	11	12	13	14	15
16	17	18	19	20	21	22
23	24	25	26	27	28	29
30	31					

TUESDAY 4
Shrove Tuesday

WEDNESDAY 5
Ash Wednesday
Islamic New Year (1424)

THURSDAY 6

FRIDAY 7

SATURDAY 8

SUNDAY 9

March

MONDAY 10
Commonwealth Day

TUESDAY 11
◐ (First Quarter)

WEDNESDAY 12

THURSDAY 13

FRIDAY 14

SATURDAY 15

SUNDAY 16

March

S	M	T	W	T	F	S
						1
2	3	4	5	6	7	8
9	10	11	12	13	14	15
16	17	18	19	20	21	22
23	24	25	26	27	28	29
30	31					

March

MONDAY 17
St. Patrick's Day Holiday (Ireland)
Canberra Day (Aus)

Weeks 12 – 13

TUESDAY 18
○ (Full Moon)

WEDNESDAY 19

THURSDAY 20
Vernal Equinox

FRIDAY 21
Human Rights Day (South Africa)

SATURDAY 22

SUNDAY 23

March

S	M	T	W	T	F	S
						1
2	3	4	5	6	7	8
9	10	11	12	13	14	15
16	17	18	19	20	21	22
23	24	25	26	27	28	29
30	31					

March

MONDAY 24

TUESDAY 25
◐ (Last Quarter)

WEDNESDAY 26

THURSDAY 27

FRIDAY 28

SATURDAY 29

SUNDAY 30
Mothering Sunday
British Summer Time begins

March

S	M	T	W	T	F	S
						1
2	3	4	5	6	7	8
9	10	11	12	13	14	15
16	17	18	19	20	21	22
23	24	25	26	27	28	29
30	31					

March

MONDAY 31

TUESDAY 1

● (New Moon)

WEDNESDAY 2

THURSDAY 3

Weeks 14 – 15

FRIDAY 4

SATURDAY 5

SUNDAY 6

Daylight Saving Time begins (US)

March

S	M	T	W	T	F	S
						1
2	3	4	5	6	7	8
9	10	11	12	13	14	15
16	17	18	19	20	21	22
23	24	25	26	27	28	29
30	31					

MONDAY 7

TUESDAY 8

WEDNESDAY 9
◐ (First Quarter)

THURSDAY 10

FRIDAY 11

SATURDAY 12

SUNDAY 13
Palm Sunday

April

S	M	T	W	T	F	S
		1	2	3	4	5
6	7	8	9	10	11	12
13	14	15	16	17	18	19
20	21	22	23	24	25	26
27	28	29	30			

April

THE STRANGER IN THE FOREST

The old man was too quick for him. He sprang to his feet and leaped to the top of a large rock. There he stood, grown suddenly tall, towering above them. His hood and his grey rags were flung away. His white garments shone. He lifted up his staff, and Gimli's axe leaped from his grasp and fell ringing on the ground. The sword of Aragorn, stiff in his motionless hand, blazed with a sudden fire. Legolas gave a great shout and shot an arrow high into the air: it vanished in a flash of flame.

[*The White Rider*]

April

MONDAY 14

Weeks 16 – 17

TUESDAY 15

WEDNESDAY 16
○ (Full Moon)

THURSDAY 17
First Day of Passover

FRIDAY 18
Good Friday

SATURDAY 19

SUNDAY 20
Easter Day

April

S	M	T	W	T	F	S
		1	2	3	4	5
6	7	8	9	10	11	12
13	14	15	16	17	18	19
20	21	22	23	24	25	26
27	28	29	30			

April

MONDAY 21
Easter Monday
Family Day (South Africa)

TUESDAY 22

WEDNESDAY 23
St. George's Day (England)
◐ (Last Quarter)

THURSDAY 24

FRIDAY 25
Anzac Day (Aus/NZ)

SATURDAY 26

SUNDAY 27
Freedom Day (South Africa)

April

S	M	T	W	T	F	S
		1	2	3	4	5
6	7	8	9	10	11	12
13	14	15	16	17	18	19
20	21	22	23	24	25	26
27	28	29	30			

April

MONDAY 28
Public Holiday (South Africa)

TUESDAY 29

WEDNESDAY 30

THURSDAY 1
Worker's Day (South Africa)
● (New Moon)

Weeks 18 – 19

FRIDAY 2

SATURDAY 3

SUNDAY 4

April

S	M	T	W	T	F	S
		1	2	3	4	5
6	7	8	9	10	11	12
13	14	15	16	17	18	19
20	21	22	23	24	25	26
27	28	29	30			

May

MONDAY 5
Early May Bank Holiday (UK & Rep. of Ireland)

TUESDAY 6

WEDNESDAY 7

THURSDAY 8

FRIDAY 9
◐ (First Quarter)

SATURDAY 10

SUNDAY 11
Mother's Day (US/Can/Aus/NZ)

May

S	M	T	W	T	F	S
				1	2	3
4	5	6	7	8	9	10
11	12	13	14	15	16	17
18	19	20	21	22	23	24
25	26	27	28	29	30	31

May

THE TREE SHEPHERDS

Even as he spoke, there came forward out of the trees three strange shapes. As tall as trolls they were, twelve feet or more in height; their strong bodies, stout as young trees, seemed to be clad with raiment or with hide of close-fitting grey and brown. Their limbs were long, and their hands had many fingers; their hair was stiff, and their beards grey-green as moss. They gazed out with solemn eyes, but they were not looking at the riders: their eyes were bent northwards. Suddenly they lifted their long hands to their mouths, and sent forth ringing calls, clear as notes of a horn, but more musical and various.

[*The Road to Isengard*]

May

MONDAY 12

TUESDAY 13

WEDNESDAY 14

THURSDAY 15

Weeks 20 – 21

FRIDAY 16

○ (Full Moon)

SATURDAY 17

SUNDAY 18

May

S	M	T	W	T	F	S
				1	2	3
4	5	6	7	8	9	10
11	12	13	14	15	16	17
18	19	20	21	22	23	24
25	26	27	28	29	30	31

May

MONDAY 19
Victoria Day (Can)

TUESDAY 20

WEDNESDAY 21

THURSDAY 22

FRIDAY 23
◐ (Last Quarter)

SATURDAY 24

SUNDAY 25

May

S	M	T	W	T	F	S
				1	2	3
4	5	6	7	8	9	10
11	12	13	14	15	16	17
18	19	20	21	22	23	24
25	26	27	28	29	30	31

May

MONDAY 26
Spring Bank Holiday (UK)
Memorial Day (observed) (US)

Weeks 22 – 23

TUESDAY 27

WEDNESDAY 28

THURSDAY 29

FRIDAY 30
Memorial Day

SATURDAY 31
● (New Moon)

SUNDAY 1

May

S	M	T	W	T	F	S
				1	2	3
4	5	6	7	8	9	10
11	12	13	14	15	16	17
18	19	20	21	22	23	24
25	26	27	28	29	30	31

June

MONDAY 2
Holiday (Rep. of Ireland)
Queen's Birthday (NZ)

TUESDAY 3

WEDNESDAY 4

THURSDAY 5

FRIDAY 6

SATURDAY 7
◐ (First Quarter)

SUNDAY 8
Whit Sunday

June

S	M	T	W	T	F	S
1	2	3	4	5	6	7
8	9	10	11	12	13	14
15	16	17	18	19	20	21
22	23	24	25	26	27	28
29	30					

June

THE WRATH OF THE ENTS

'**They** roared and boomed and trumpeted, until stones began to crack and fall at the mere noise of them. Merry and I lay on the ground and stuffed our cloaks into our ears. Round and round the rock of Orthanc the Ents went striding and storming like a howling gale, breaking pillars, hurling avalanches of boulders down the shafts, tossing up huge slabs of stone into the air like leaves. The tower was in the middle of a spinning whirlwind. I saw iron posts and blocks of masonry go rocketing up hundreds of feet, and smash against the windows of Orthanc.'

[*Flotsam and Jetsam*]

June

MONDAY 9
Queen's Birthday (Aus)

TUESDAY 10

WEDNESDAY 11

THURSDAY 12

Weeks 24 – 25

FRIDAY 13

SATURDAY 14
○ (Full Moon)

SUNDAY 15
Father's Day (UK & US)

June

S	M	T	W	T	F	S
1	2	3	4	5	6	7
8	9	10	11	12	13	14
15	16	17	18	19	20	21
22	23	24	25	26	27	28
29	30					

June

MONDAY 16
Youth Day (South Africa)

TUESDAY 17

WEDNESDAY 18

THURSDAY 19

FRIDAY 20

SATURDAY 21
Summer Solstice
◐ (Last Quarter)

SUNDAY 22

June

S	M	T	W	T	F	S
1	2	3	4	5	6	7
8	9	10	11	12	13	14
15	16	17	18	19	20	21
22	23	24	25	26	27	28
29	30					

June

MONDAY 23

TUESDAY 24

WEDNESDAY 25

THURSDAY 26

Weeks 26 – 27

FRIDAY 27

SATURDAY 28

SUNDAY 29

● (New Moon)

June

S	M	T	W	T	F	S
1	2	3	4	5	6	7
8	9	10	11	12	13	14
15	16	17	18	19	20	21
22	23	24	25	26	27	28
29	30					

July

MONDAY 30

TUESDAY 1
Canada Day (Can)

WEDNESDAY 2

THURSDAY 3

FRIDAY 4
Independence Day (US)

SATURDAY 5

SUNDAY 6

July

S	M	T	W	T	F	S
		1	2	3	4	5
6	7	8	9	10	11	12
13	14	15	16	17	18	19
20	21	22	23	24	25	26
27	28	29	30	31		

July

APPARITIONS

Presently it grew altogether dark: the air itself seemed black and heavy to breathe. When lights appeared Sam rubbed his eyes: he thought his head was going queer. He first saw one with the corner of his left eye, a wisp of pale sheen that faded away; but others appeared soon after: some like dimly shining smoke, some like misty flames flickering slowly above unseen candles; here and there they twisted like ghostly sheets unfurled by hidden hands. But neither of his companions spoke a word.

At last Sam could bear it no longer. 'What's all this, Gollum?' he said in a whisper.

[*The Passage of the Marshes*]

Ted Nasmith 01

July

MONDAY 7
◐ (First Quarter)

Weeks 28 – 29

TUESDAY 8

WEDNESDAY 9

THURSDAY 10

FRIDAY 11

SATURDAY 12
Battle of the Boyne Holiday (N.Ireland)

SUNDAY 13
○ (Full Moon)

July

S	M	T	W	T	F	S
		1	2	3	4	5
6	7	8	9	10	11	12
13	14	15	16	17	18	19
20	21	22	23	24	25	26
27	28	29	30	31		

July

MONDAY 14

TUESDAY 15

WEDNESDAY 16

THURSDAY 17

FRIDAY 18

SATURDAY 19

SUNDAY 20

July

S	M	T	W	T	F	S
		1	2	3	4	5
6	7	8	9	10	11	12
13	14	15	16	17	18	19
20	21	22	23	24	25	26
27	28	29	30	31		

July

MONDAY 21
◐ (Last Quarter)

TUESDAY 22

WEDNESDAY 23

THURSDAY 24

Weeks 30 – 31

FRIDAY 25

SATURDAY 26

SUNDAY 27

July

S	M	T	W	T	F	S
		1	2	3	4	5
6	7	8	9	10	11	12
13	14	15	16	17	18	19
20	21	22	23	24	25	26
27	28	29	30	31		

August

MONDAY 28

TUESDAY 29

The Fellowship of the Ring first published, 1954

● (New Moon)

WEDNESDAY 30

THURSDAY 31

FRIDAY 1

SATURDAY 2

SUNDAY 3

August

S	M	T	W	T	F	S
					1	2
3	4	5	6	7	8	9
10	11	12	13	14	15	16
17	18	19	20	21	22	23
24	25	26	27	28	29	30
31						

August

FIRST SIGHT OF ITHILIEN

Day was opening in the sky, and they saw that the mountains were now much further off, receding eastward in a long curve that was lost in the distance. Before them, as they turned west, gentle slopes ran down into dim hazes far below. All about them were small woods of resinous trees, fir and cedar and cypress, and other kinds unknown in the Shire, with wide glades among them; and everywhere there was a wealth of sweet-smelling herbs and shrubs... Here Spring was already busy about them: fronds pierced moss and mould, larches were green-fingered, small flowers were opening in the turf, birds were singing. Ithilien, the garden of Gondor now desolate kept still a dishevelled dryad loveliness.

[*Of Herbs and Stewed Rabbit*]

August

MONDAY 4
Holiday (Scotland & Rep. of Ireland)
Civic Holiday (Can)

TUESDAY 5
◐ (First Quarter)

WEDNESDAY 6

THURSDAY 7

Weeks 32 – 33

FRIDAY 8

SATURDAY 9
National Women's Day (South Africa)

SUNDAY 10

August

S	M	T	W	T	F	S
					1	2
3	4	5	6	7	8	9
10	11	12	13	14	15	16
17	18	19	20	21	22	23
24	25	26	27	28	29	30
31						

August

MONDAY 11

TUESDAY 12

○ (Full Moon)

WEDNESDAY 13

THURSDAY 14

FRIDAY 15

SATURDAY 16

SUNDAY 17

August

S	M	T	W	T	F	S
					1	2
3	4	5	6	7	8	9
10	11	12	13	14	15	16
17	18	19	20	21	22	23
24	25	26	27	28	29	30
31						

August

MONDAY 18

TUESDAY 19

WEDNESDAY 20
◐ (Last Quarter)

THURSDAY 21

Weeks 34 – 35

FRIDAY 22

SATURDAY 23

SUNDAY 24

August

S	M	T	W	T	F	S
					1	2
3	4	5	6	7	8	9
10	11	12	13	14	15	16
17	18	19	20	21	22	23
24	25	26	27	28	29	30
31						

August

MONDAY 25
Summer Bank Holiday (UK)

TUESDAY 26

WEDNESDAY 27
● (New Moon)

THURSDAY 28

FRIDAY 29

SATURDAY 30

SUNDAY 31

August

S	M	T	W	T	F	S
					1	2
3	4	5	6	7	8	9
10	11	12	13	14	15	16
17	18	19	20	21	22	23
24	25	26	27	28	29	30
31						

September

THE MÛMAK OF HARAD

TO his astonishment and terror, and lasting delight, Sam saw a vast shape crash out of the trees and come careering down the slope. Big as a house, much bigger than a house, it looked to him, a grey-clad moving hill. Fear and wonder, maybe, enlarged him in the hobbit's eyes, but the Mûmak of Harad was indeed a beast of vast bulk, and the like of him does not walk now in Middle-earth... On he came, straight towards the watchers, and then swerved aside in the nick of time, passing only a few yards away, rocking the ground beneath their feet: his great legs like trees, enormous sail-like ears spread out, long snout upraised like a huge serpent about to strike, his small red eyes raging. His upturned hornlike tusks were bound with bands of gold and dripped with blood... and high upon his neck still desperately clung a tiny figure – the body of a mighty warrior, a giant among the Swertings.

[*Of Herbs and Stewed Rabbit*]

Nasmith 1994

September

MONDAY 1
Labor Day (US & Can)

TUESDAY 2
J.R.R. Tolkien died, 1973

WEDNESDAY 3
◐ (First Quarter)

THURSDAY 4

Weeks 36 – 37

FRIDAY 5

SATURDAY 6

SUNDAY 7
Father's Day (Aus & NZ)

September

S	M	T	W	T	F	S
	1	2	3	4	5	6
7	8	9	10	11	12	13
14	15	16	17	18	19	20
21	22	23	24	25	26	27
28	29	30				

September

MONDAY 8

TUESDAY 9

WEDNESDAY 10
○ (Full Moon)

THURSDAY 11

FRIDAY 12

SATURDAY 13

SUNDAY 14

September

S	M	T	W	T	F	S
	1	2	3	4	5	6
7	8	9	10	11	12	13
14	15	16	17	18	19	20
21	22	23	24	25	26	27
28	29	30				

September

MONDAY 15
The Silmarillion first published, 1977

TUESDAY 16

WEDNESDAY 17

THURSDAY 18
◐ (Last Quarter)

Weeks 38 – 39

FRIDAY 19

SATURDAY 20

SUNDAY 21
The Hobbit first published, 1937

September

S	M	T	W	T	F	S
	1	2	3	4	5	6
7	8	9	10	11	12	13
14	15	16	17	18	19	20
21	22	23	24	25	26	27
28	29	30				

September

MONDAY 22

TUESDAY 23
Autumnal Equinox

WEDNESDAY 24
Heritage Day (South Africa)

THURSDAY 25

FRIDAY 26
● (New Moon)

SATURDAY 27
Rosh Hashanah

SUNDAY 28

September

S	M	T	W	T	F	S
	1	2	3	4	5	6
7	8	9	10	11	12	13
14	15	16	17	18	19	20
21	22	23	24	25	26	27
28	29	30				

September

MONDAY 29

TUESDAY 30

WEDNESDAY 1

THURSDAY 2

Unfinished Tales first published, 1980

◐ (First Quarter)

Weeks 40 – 41

FRIDAY 3

SATURDAY 4

SUNDAY 5

September

S	M	T	W	T	F	S
	1	2	3	4	5	6
7	8	9	10	11	12	13
14	15	16	17	18	19	20
21	22	23	24	25	26	27
28	29	30				

October

MONDAY 6
Yom Kippur

TUESDAY 7

WEDNESDAY 8

THURSDAY 9

FRIDAY 10
○ (Full Moon)

SATURDAY 11

SUNDAY 12

October

S	M	T	W	T	F	S
			1	2	3	4
5	6	7	8	9	10	11
12	13	14	15	16	17	18
19	20	21	22	23	24	25
26	27	28	29	30	31	

October

THE TERRACE AT HENNETH ANNÛN

At last they came out of the stony darkness and looked about. They were on a wide flat rock without rail or parapet. At their right, eastwards, the torrent fell, splashing over many terraces, and then, pouring down a steep race, it filled a smooth-hewn channel with a dark force of water flecked with foam, and curling and rushing almost at their feet it plunged sheer over the edge that yawned upon their left. A man stood there, near the brink, silent, gazing down.

[*The Forbidden Pool*]

October

MONDAY 13
Columbus Day (US)
Thanksgiving Day (Can)

TUESDAY 14

WEDNESDAY 15

THURSDAY 16

Weeks 42 – 43

FRIDAY 17

SATURDAY 18
◐ (Last Quarter)

SUNDAY 19

October

S	M	T	W	T	F	S
			1	2	3	4
5	6	7	8	9	10	11
12	13	14	15	16	17	18
19	20	21	22	23	24	25
26	27	28	29	30	31	

October

MONDAY 20
The Return of the King first published, 1955

TUESDAY 21

WEDNESDAY 22

THURSDAY 23

FRIDAY 24
United Nations Day

SATURDAY 25
Diwali
● (New Moon)

SUNDAY 26
British Summer Time ends
Daylight Saving Time ends (US)

October

S	M	T	W	T	F	S
			1	2	3	4
5	6	7	8	9	10	11
12	13	14	15	16	17	18
19	20	21	22	23	24	25
26	27	28	29	30	31	

October

MONDAY 27
Holiday (Rep. of Ireland)
First Day of Ramadan
Labour Day (NZ)

Weeks 44 – 45

TUESDAY 28

WEDNESDAY 29

THURSDAY 30

FRIDAY 31
Hallowe'en

SATURDAY 1
All Saints' Day
◐ (First Quarter)

SUNDAY 2

October

S	M	T	W	T	F	S
			1	2	3	4
5	6	7	8	9	10	11
12	13	14	15	16	17	18
19	20	21	22	23	24	25
26	27	28	29	30	31	

November

MONDAY 3

TUESDAY 4
Election Day (US)

WEDNESDAY 5

THURSDAY 6

FRIDAY 7

SATURDAY 8

SUNDAY 9
Remembrance Day (UK & Commonwealth)
○ (Full Moon)

November

S	M	T	W	T	F	S
						1
2	3	4	5	6	7	8
9	10	11	12	13	14	15
16	17	18	19	20	21	22
23	24	25	26	27	28	29
30						

November

AT THE CROSS-ROADS

'The brief glow fell upon a huge sitting figure, still and solemn as the great stone kings of Argonath. The years had gnawed it, and violent hands had maimed it. Its head was gone, and in its place was set in mockery a round rough-hewn stone, rudely painted by savage hands in the likeness of a grinning face with one large red eye in the midst of its forehead. Upon its knees and mighty chair, and all about the pedestal, were idle scrawls mixed with the foul symbols that the maggot-folk of Mordor used.

Suddenly, caught by the level beams, Frodo saw the old king's head: it was lying rolled away by the roadside. 'Look, Sam!' he cried, startled into speech. 'Look! The king has got a crown again!'

[*Journey to the Cross-roads*]

November

MONDAY 10

TUESDAY 11

The Two Towers first published, 1954
Veterans' Day (US)
Remembrance Day (Can)

WEDNESDAY 12

THURSDAY 13

Weeks 46 – 47

FRIDAY 14

SATURDAY 15

SUNDAY 16

November

S	M	T	W	T	F	S
						1
2	3	4	5	6	7	8
9	10	11	12	13	14	15
16	17	18	19	20	21	22
23	24	25	26	27	28	29
30						

November

MONDAY 17
◐ (Last Quarter)

TUESDAY 18

WEDNESDAY 19

THURSDAY 20

FRIDAY 21

SATURDAY 22

SUNDAY 23
● (New Moon)

November

S	M	T	W	T	F	S
						1
2	3	4	5	6	7	8
9	10	11	12	13	14	15
16	17	18	19	20	21	22
23	24	25	26	27	28	29
30						

November

MONDAY 24

TUESDAY 25
Eid-al-Fitr

WEDNESDAY 26

THURSDAY 27
Thanksgiving Day (US)

Weeks 48 – 49

FRIDAY 28

SATURDAY 29

SUNDAY 30
St. Andrew's Day (Scotland)
◐ (First Quarter)

November

S	M	T	W	T	F	S
						1
2	3	4	5	6	7	8
9	10	11	12	13	14	15
16	17	18	19	20	21	22
23	24	25	26	27	28	29
30						

December

MONDAY 1

TUESDAY 2

WEDNESDAY 3

THURSDAY 4

FRIDAY 5

SATURDAY 6

SUNDAY 7

December

S	M	T	W	T	F	S
	1	2	3	4	5	6
7	8	9	10	11	12	13
14	15	16	17	18	19	20
21	22	23	24	25	26	27
28	29	30	31			

December

THE TOWER OF THE MOON

A long-tilted valley, a deep gulf of shadow, ran back far into the mountains. Upon the further side, some way within the valley's arms, high on a rocky seat upon the black knees of the Ephel Dúath, stood the walls and tower of Minas Morgul. All was dark about it, earth and sky, but it was lit with light. Not the imprisoned moonlight welling through the marble walls of Minas Ithil long ago, Tower of the Moon, fair and radiant in the hollow of the hills. Paler indeed than the moon ailing in some slow eclipse was the light of it now, wavering and blowing like a noisome exhalation of decay, a corpse-light, a light that illuminated nothing.

[*The Stairs of Cirith Ungol*]

Ted Nasmith

December

MONDAY 8
○ (Full Moon)

TUESDAY 9

WEDNESDAY 10

THURSDAY 11

Weeks 50 – 51

FRIDAY 12

SATURDAY 13

SUNDAY 14

December

S	M	T	W	T	F	S
	1	2	3	4	5	6
7	8	9	10	11	12	13
14	15	16	17	18	19	20
21	22	23	24	25	26	27
28	29	30	31			

December

MONDAY 15

TUESDAY 16
Day of Reconciliation (South Africa)
◐ (Last Quarter)

WEDNESDAY 17

THURSDAY 18

FRIDAY 19

SATURDAY 20
First Day of Hanukkah

SUNDAY 21

December

S	M	T	W	T	F	S
	1	2	3	4	5	6
7	8	9	10	11	12	13
14	15	16	17	18	19	20
21	22	23	24	25	26	27
28	29	30	31			

December

MONDAY 22
Winter Solstice

TUESDAY 23
● (New Moon)

WEDNESDAY 24

THURSDAY 25
Christmas Day

Weeks 52 – 53

FRIDAY 26
Boxing Day
St. Stephen's Day (Rep. of Ireland)
Day of Goodwill (South Africa)

SATURDAY 27

SUNDAY 28

December

S	M	T	W	T	F	S
	1	2	3	4	5	6
7	8	9	10	11	12	13
14	15	16	17	18	19	20
21	22	23	24	25	26	27
28	29	30	31			

January 2004

MONDAY 29

TUESDAY 30
◐ (First Quarter)

WEDNESDAY 31

THURSDAY 1
New Year's Day

FRIDAY 2

SATURDAY 3
J.R.R. Tolkien born 1892

SUNDAY 4

January

S	M	T	W	T	F	S
				1	2	3
4	5	6	7	8	9	10
11	12	13	14	15	16	17
18	19	20	21	22	23	24
25	26	27	28	29	30	31

2004

SHELOB'S RETREAT

As if his indomitable spirit had set its potency in motion, the glass blazed suddenly like a white torch in his hand. It flamed like a star that leaping from the firmament sears the dark air with intolerable light. No such terror out of heaven had ever burned in Shelob's face before. The beams of it entered into her wounded head and scored it with unbearable pain, and the dreadful infection of light spread from eye to eye. She fell back beating the air with her forelegs, her sight blasted by inner lightnings, her mind in agony. Then turning her maimed head away, she rolled aside and began to crawl, claw by claw, towards the opening in the dark cliff behind.

[*The Choices of Master Samwise*]

Ted Nasmith

NOTES & ADDRESSES

NOTES & ADDRESSES

2003

JANUARY

S	M	T	W	T	F	S
			1	2	3	4
5	6	7	8	9	10	11
12	13	14	15	16	17	18
19	20	21	22	23	24	25
26	27	28	29	30	31	

FEBRUARY

S	M	T	W	T	F	S
						1
2	3	4	5	6	7	8
9	10	11	12	13	14	15
16	17	18	19	20	21	22
23	24	25	26	27	28	

MARCH

S	M	T	W	T	F	S
						1
2	3	4	5	6	7	8
9	10	11	12	13	14	15
16	17	18	19	20	21	22
23	24	25	26	27	28	29
30	31					

APRIL

S	M	T	W	T	F	S
		1	2	3	4	5
6	7	8	9	10	11	12
13	14	15	16	17	18	19
20	21	22	23	24	25	26
27	28	29	30			

MAY

S	M	T	W	T	F	S
				1	2	3
4	5	6	7	8	9	10
11	12	13	14	15	16	17
18	19	20	21	22	23	24
25	26	27	28	29	30	31

JUNE

S	M	T	W	T	F	S
1	2	3	4	5	6	7
8	9	10	11	12	13	14
15	16	17	18	19	20	21
22	23	24	25	26	27	28
29	30					

JULY

S	M	T	W	T	F	S
		1	2	3	4	5
6	7	8	9	10	11	12
13	14	15	16	17	18	19
20	21	22	23	24	25	26
27	28	29	30	31		

AUGUST

S	M	T	W	T	F	S
					1	2
3	4	5	6	7	8	9
10	11	12	13	14	15	16
17	18	19	20	21	22	23
24	25	26	27	28	29	30
31						

SEPTEMBER

S	M	T	W	T	F	S
	1	2	3	4	5	6
7	8	9	10	11	12	13
14	15	16	17	18	19	20
21	22	23	24	25	26	27
28	29	30				

OCTOBER

S	M	T	W	T	F	S
			1	2	3	4
5	6	7	8	9	10	11
12	13	14	15	16	17	18
19	20	21	22	23	24	25
26	27	28	29	30	31	

NOVEMBER

S	M	T	W	T	F	S
						1
2	3	4	5	6	7	8
9	10	11	12	13	14	15
16	17	18	19	20	21	22
23	24	25	26	27	28	29
30						

DECEMBER

S	M	T	W	T	F	S
	1	2	3	4	5	6
7	8	9	10	11	12	13
14	15	16	17	18	19	20
21	22	23	24	25	26	27
28	29	30	31			